Contents

For attention of the learner

You are not allowed to copy any information from this book and use it as your own evidence. That would count as plagiarism, which is taken very seriously and may result in disqualification. If you are in any doubt at all please speak to your teacher.

Command words

You will find the following command words in the assessment criteria for each unit. These descriptions may help you to understand what you have to submit for each Pass, Merit and Distinction grading criterion.

Outline	Write a clear description but not a detailed one.
Explain	Set out in detail the meaning of something, with reasons. More difficult than 'describe' or 'list', so it can help to give an example to show what you mean. Start by introducing the topic then give the 'how' or 'why'.
Compare	Identify the main factors that apply in two or more situations and explain the similarities and differences or advantages and disadvantages.
Assess	Give careful consideration to all the factors or events that apply and identify which are the most important or relevant.
Describe	Give a clear description that includes all the relevant features - think of it as 'painting a picture with words'.
Justify	Give reasons or evidence to support your opinion or view and show how you arrived at these conclusions.

BTEC BUSINESS

ASSESSMENT GUIDE

Unit 7 PROVIDING BUSINESS SUPPORT

CAROLE TROTTER

HODDER
EDUCATION
AN HACHETTE UK COMPANY

The sample learner answers provided in this assessment guide are intended to give guidance on how a learner might approach generating evidence for each assessment criterion. Answers do not necessarily include all of the evidence required to meet each assessment criterion. Assessor comments intend to highlight how sample answers might be improved to help learners meet the requirements of the grading criterion but are provided as a guide only. Sample answers and assessor guidance have not been verified by Edexcel and any information provided in this guide should not replace your own internal verification process.

Any work submitted as evidence for assessment for this unit must be the learner's own. Submitting as evidence, in whole or in part, any material taken from this guide will be regarded as plagiarism. Hodder Education accepts no responsibility for learners plagiarising work from this guide that does or does not meet the assessment criteria.

The sample assignment briefs are provided as a guide to how you might assess the evidence required for all or part of the internal assessment of this Unit. They have not been verified or endorsed by Edexcel and should be internally verified through your own Lead Internal Verifier as with any other assignment briefs, and/or checked through the BTEC assignment checking service.

Orders: please contact Bookpoint Ltd, 130 Milton Park, Abingdon, Oxon OX14 4SB. Telephone: (44) 01235 827720. Fax: (44) 01235 400454. Lines are open from 9.00 to 5.00, Monday to Saturday, with a 24-hour message answering service. You can also order through our website www.hoddereducation.co.uk

If you have any comments to make about this, or any of our other titles, please send them to educationenquiries@hodder.co.uk

British Library Cataloguing in Publication Data

A catalogue record for this title is available from the British Library

ISBN: 978 1444 18692 5

This edition published 2013

Impression number   10 9 8 7 6 5 4 3 2 1

Year   2016, 2015, 2014, 2013

Copyright © 2013 Carole Trotter

Cover photo from © mybaitshop – Fotolia

Typeset by Integra Software Services Pvt. Ltd., Pondicherry, India.

Printed in Dubai for Hodder Education,
An Hachette UK Company,
338 Euston Road,
London NW1 3BH

Introduction

Unit 7, Providing Business Support, is an internally assessed specialist optional unit with three learning aims. It focuses on the roles and functions which provide support for a business. The unit identifies the equipment used to provide support for the business and how it should be used both efficiently and safely. The final part of this unit is an introduction to the tasks and activities that need to be completed before, during and following a meeting.

This unit also provides an opportunity to plan and participate in a meeting.

This book includes:

- Guidance on each learning aim – all the topics in the learning aims should be studied, and the book includes useful suggestions for each. Examples are included, but these could be replaced by local examples from your area.
- Evidence generated by a learner for each assessment criterion, with feedback from an assessor. The assessor has highlighted where the evidence is sufficient to satisfy the grading criterion, and provided developmental feedback when additional work is required. This material provides support for assessment.
- Examples of assignment briefs, with clear guidance on the evidence you will need to generate and submit for each grading criterion, and the format in which the evidence should be submitted.

Answers to the knowledge recap questions provided in the learning aim summaries can be found at the back of the guide.

Learning aim A
Understand the purpose of providing business support

Learning aim A provides the opportunity to get a better understanding of the activities and tasks which provide support for a business and to understand the purpose of business support.

Assessment criteria

2A.P1 Explain the purpose of different types of business support in two contrasting businesses.

Topic A.1 Types of support

There are a lot of activities which need to be implemented effectively for a business to operate efficiently.

Dealing with visitors

Studied ☐

The employee whose role it is to welcome visitors is responsible for creating a good first impression. They must be friendly, polite and have excellent verbal and non-verbal communication skills. Dealing with visitors will involve:

- welcoming and greeting the visitor
- logging visitor details and if relevant providing name badges
- providing the visitor with accurate information
- dealing efficiently with problems
- showing the visitor to facilities or a meeting room
- arranging car parking or taxis.

Organising travel and accommodation

Studied ☐

The employee responsible for organising travel and accommodation bookings needs to be organised and efficient. They will be responsible for:

- understanding the itinerary, budget and any special requirements
- booking appropriate travel and hotel arrangements to match the dates on the itinerary
- communicating professionally, accurately and clearly

Figure 1.1 Organising travel is an important aspect of business support

- collating and checking travel documents, visas and hotel confirmations
- keeping records
- dealing with any problems
- evaluating the accommodation for quality and facilities for any future visits.

Managing diaries

A diary system should schedule business activities, meetings and appointments. To be effective, entries need to be up to date and secure. Electronic diaries allow you to share information, identify convenient times for meetings, know the whereabouts of staff and prioritise activities. They can provide reminder prompts when important tasks need to be completed and when external meetings are due.

Using telephone systems to make, receive and transfer calls

The telephone allows a business to communicate with both existing and potential customers. Good telephone skills are important for the success of the business and these will include:

- presenting a positive image of the business
- following the business procedure for answering the telephone
- having the correct information available when making a call
- answering promptly and politely – introducing self and the business
- finding out what the caller wants
- providing information or transferring the call to the relevant person
- taking and recording accurate messages
- logging all calls.

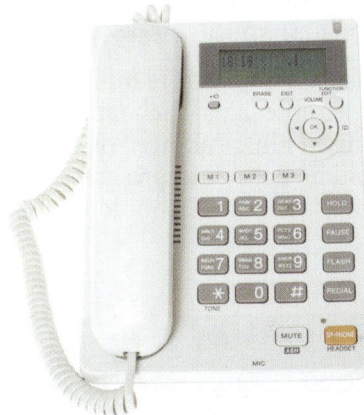

Figure 1.2 Good telephone skills present a positive image of the business

Organising and supporting meetings

For a meeting to run smoothly, a lot of activities need to be planned and coordinated.

Before the meeting the purpose, time and date should be agreed, the agenda prepared and delegates contacted. A room should be booked and all resources and refreshments organised. Delegates should be provided with a copy of the agenda, directions to the meeting location and any other relevant documents. Attendance should be confirmed.

At the meeting all equipment should be checked. Delegates should be welcomed and their attendance recorded. Notes should be taken on the main discussion points and agreed actions.

After the meeting the room should be left clean and tidy and any spare documents removed. The minutes should be produced, checked and circulated.

Producing documents

Studied ☐

All documents must be clear, accurate and provide sufficient information. They should be professional, follow house style and have accurate spelling and grammar. Documents should comply with legislation such as the Data Protection Act.

Processing and storing information, both manually and electronically

Studied ☐

When processing information the business must make sure that the sources are accurate and up to date. All documents should be organised and stored securely in an appropriate format, and so that they can be found easily. A business should have clear procedures for who has access to what information and how and when information should be archived. All collection and storage of information must comply with the Data Protection Act.

A business could store information in a manual filing system (for example, an alphabetically, numerically or chronologically organised filing cabinet), or electronically on a computer (files should be password protected, archived and backed-up as appropriate). There should be clear procedures for the deletion or disposal of files.

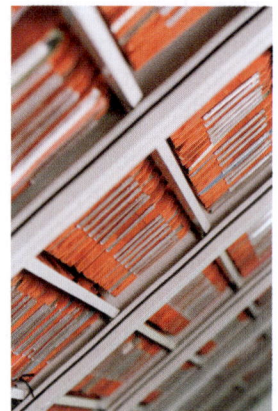

Figure 1.3 A manual filing system

✔ Topic A.1 Knowledge recap questions

1. Why would an administrator need access to the itinerary to book travel and accommodation for managers or colleagues?

2. What are the benefits of a business implementing a set procedure for answering the phone?

3. What are the benefits of having an electronic diary system rather than a paper-based one?

Topic A.2 The purpose of providing business support

To be successful a business will rely heavily on the efficiency of several business support processes. Accurate records, effective communication and good organisation will help the business make decisions quickly and remain competitive.

Ensuring consistency

The service provided by a business must be consistently efficient and of a high standard or customers and suppliers will move their custom elsewhere. Any documents or company resources must portray a consistent positive image and one that customers and suppliers link to trust and quality.

Making effective use of time

Well-organised diaries and efficiently planned travel arrangements will allow staff to be well prepared to meet potential customers or suppliers. Well-organised filing systems will prevent time being lost searching for information. Effective use of time will enable a business to prioritise activities, meet deadlines and stay competitive.

Providing support for managers, teams, colleagues and departmental processes

Business support processes can:

- manage diaries so that managers know when employees are at meetings; regularly update the diary so that all staff know about any changes to team or departmental meetings; and prioritise events and set reminders for colleagues in electronic diaries
- produce professional and clear documents in the house style
- meet and greet visitors in a welcoming and professional manner
- make travel and accommodation bookings which match itinerary requirements; and check the price and quality of accommodation
- make preparations and arrangements for meetings and produce relevant documentation
- maintain a log of visitors and telephone calls
- maintain an effective filing system
- provide telephone support and record accurate messages when staff are not available.

Providing effective service to internal and external customers

The business support process can provide effective service to internal and external customers by:

- having up-to-date information on products
- having knowledge of individual customer needs and expectations
- using clear and efficient communication channels
- creating professional documents with all the relevant information and no jargon
- supporting customers with problems, queries and complaints
- following up on complaints.

Figure 1.4 Businesses should support customers with any queries or complaints

Topic A.2 Knowledge recap questions

1. Identify two ways a manager would benefit from using business support.
2. Why is it important for the business support process to be effective when dealing with external customers?

Assessment guidance for learning aim A

2A.P1 Explain the purpose of different types of business support in two contrasting businesses

✏️ Learner answer

> The businesses I have chosen to use are AT Engineering, a local private limited company which supplies and maintains equipment for other businesses and The Rink, a local leisure centre. I have chosen to use these two businesses because I did my first work placement in the office at AT Engineering and I am currently doing a work placement at The Rink.

Assessor report: The command verb for 2A.P1 is **explain**; to achieve this the learner will need to set out in detail, with reasons, the purpose of the different types of business support for two businesses. It can help to give an example to show what you mean. Start by introducing the topic then give the 'how' or 'why'.

The learner has made a good choice by selecting to provide evidence on two contrasting businesses that they know well.

✏️ Learner answer

> AT Engineering has an administrator who provides the following types of business support:
> - Word processes letters, reports and invoices
> - Answers the telephone and takes messages
> - Keeps manual files up to date
> - Welcomes visitors
> - Makes arrangements for meetings.
>
> The office staff at The Rink provide the following types of business support:
>
> - Preparing documents in Word, Excel and Publisher
> - Answering the telephone, taking messages

- Photocopying documents
- Keeping diaries for senior managers updated
- Making arrangements for meetings
- Making arrangements for travel and accommodation.

Assessor report: The learner has currently just **listed** the tasks carried out by the administrator at AT Engineering and the office staff at The Rink. The learner will now need to explain the purpose of the business support activities.

✎ Learner answer

The administrator for AT Engineering produces all documents (letters, reports, meeting agendas, minutes and invoices) in the house style, which shows the company logo and corporate colours. There are templates for the documents on the computer. These look neat and professional and save time because a lot of information is already on the templates. Computer documents can be checked for spelling and grammar errors. If the administrator is unsure of the content for letters they can forward them by email to their line manager or a senior manager to check they are accurate.

There are computer files for customers and suppliers but there is also a filing cabinet with paper files on all current and past customers and suppliers and their products and price lists. Documents are filed in alphabetical order by the customers' and suppliers' surnames, so they can be found quickly and easily.

All visitors are met and welcomed by the administrator at the front entrance and are asked to sign the visitor book. The administrator is required to dress smartly as this creates a good first impression and image for the business. The administrator is responsible for promptly letting managers know that their visitors have arrived and for providing refreshments for the visitor. This makes the visitors feel valued and gives a good impression of the business.

The business has a telephone procedure which must be followed. All calls must be answered promptly; the administrator is required to give the name of the business and her name. All calls are logged and logged sheets are filed away at the end of the week. Messages are recorded and passed on as soon as possible. The message pad records when and who the message was given to so there is a record on who is dealing with any problems or issues.

The administrator is responsible for preparing the documents for meetings and sending out agendas and minutes. The senior managers will provide the information for the meeting. The administrator will make all the arrangements so that the relevant people know why they are meeting and are in the correct location and at the right time.

Assessor report: The learner has provided a good explanation of the purpose of the administrator word processing documents, keeping files up to date and welcoming visitors.

Assessor report – overall

Is the evidence sufficient to satisfy the grading criterion?

In the first section the learner has clearly identified why the two businesses were selected. The learner has submitted a list of the types of business support for each business and has developed this by explaining how and why AT Engineering uses the business support processes listed. The learner has currently just submitted a list of the business support processes at The Rink with no explanation.

What additional evidence, if any, is required?

To achieve 2A.P1 the learner will need to explain the purpose of the different types of business support at The Rink.

Learning aim B
Use office equipment safely for different purposes

Learning aim B provides an introduction to the equipment that is required to provide support for a business and how that equipment should be used safely.

Assessment criteria

2B.P2	Describe the use of office equipment to meet different business requirements.
2B.P3	Demonstrate using office equipment safely, in accordance with health and safety legislation.
2B.M1	Explain the appropriate uses of office equipment types, features and functions to suit different business purposes.
2B.M2	Demonstrate understanding of the application of safe lifting techniques when using office equipment.
2B.D1	Analyse the contribution that office equipment makes to the provision of business support.

Topic B.1 Office equipment

Most businesses rely on a range of office equipment to operate and function efficiently.

Types

Studied ☐

The main types of equipment are:

- **Computer** – to communicate with customers, suppliers and colleagues by letter or email; to create cash flow forecasts, charts and graphs; to manage customer and supplier accounts; to produce presentations; to produce marketing or promotional material; to trade online
- **Printer** – to produce professional-looking documents in black and white or colour
- **Photocopier** – to produce multiple copies of a document or to enlarge or reduce the size of images
- **Telephone system** – to communicate with customers, suppliers and colleagues
- **Office chair** – this should be comfortable, adjustable and comply with any health and safety requirements.

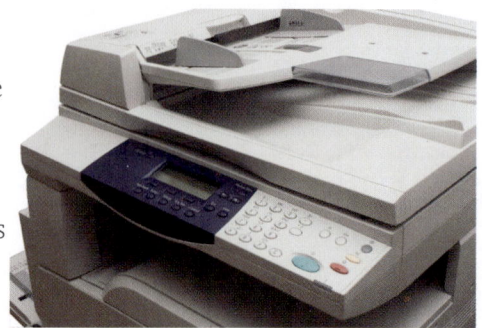

Figure 2.1 Having the right equipment can help a business operate more efficiently

Features and functions

Studied

To use equipment efficiently and effectively the user needs to understand its features and functions. Training should be provided so that employees know how to use equipment correctly.

The type of equipment purchased will depend on the size of the business and what the equipment is being used for. A small business may only need a basic computer and software package for word processing and spreadsheets. A larger business will need a computer with more memory and advanced software packages to cope with more customer and supplier records and financial data and may also need software to design promotional material.

A printer needs to produce clear documents. A business may use a laser printer which is quiet and quick and which, over time, will cost less to print per page; or an inkjet printer, which is often smaller and cheaper to buy. The user can select to print all or selected sections of a document, and can choose to print only on one side or on both sides of the paper.

Photocopiers could produce only black and white copies or colour copies as well. They can reduce or enlarge documents and many have additional features such as producing two-sided copies, collating, punching holes or stapling.

Telephone systems could have features such as transferring calls to another colleague or department, playing music or advertisements when the caller is on hold, caller ID, voicemail and teleconferencing.

Office chairs should be comfortable and safe for the user as specified in the Health and Safety (Display Screen Equipment) Regulations 1992. They should have adjustable heights and sufficient back support.

Figure 2.2 Chairs are an important part of office equipment

Instruction manuals

Studied

It is important that those using equipment read the instruction manual to ensure they know how to use it correctly. The manual will provide guidance on how to set up and use the equipment and solutions for minor problems. Using equipment correctly will maximise efficiency and reduce time lost in waiting for maintenance and repairs. Incorrect use of the equipment could incur costly repair bills, disruption to work procedures, inability to meet deadlines or commitments and unnecessary waste of resources. The manufacturer's instruction manuals could be used as part of the training package to help employees fully utilise the equipment and to prevent any health or safety issues.

Training in usage of equipment

Studied ☐

Employees should be provided with appropriate training in the correct and safe usage of the equipment. Employees who have been appropriately trained are more likely to produce work which is of a high standard; they will have increased job knowledge and skills which will improve motivation and may result in promotion. Resources wastage will be kept to a minimum, staff will meet deadlines, there will be no unnecessary repair bills and the likelihood of accidents will be reduced.

Problem solving

Studied ☐

A business can install the most up-to-date equipment and implement training for staff, but the equipment could still develop problems and break down. This can cause disruption to workplace activities and stress for the user. The business should purchase good quality products which are capable of coping with the workload to avoid incurring costly repair bills. All equipment should have regular maintenance checks.

If staff have good knowledge of the equipment and are appropriately trained they should be able to solve minor problems such as paper jams or replacing print cartridges.

It is important to follow manufacturers' instructions and organisational procedures when dealing with equipment faults. All users must know the procedure for reporting and logging problems and know their boundaries for dealing with problems.

Meeting different business requirements

Studied ☐

Buying any equipment is a cost to the business and the equipment must meet the different business requirements. The type and size of the business will affect the type of equipment required, but it is essential that the equipment can do the job it was purchased to do. When purchasing printers and photocopiers the business will need to consider the volume of work involved and the quality they require for the printed copies.

Topic B.1 Knowledge recap questions ✓

1. What are the benefits to the business of providing employees with training on how to use office equipment?

2. Why is it important to follow the instructions in the manufacturer's manual?

3. Why should office equipment be regularly maintained?

Topic B.2 Working safely

Implementing appropriate safety measures and having appropriately trained employees will protect equipment users from having accidents and developing health problems, which in turn will prevent sick leave, lost working hours, insurance claims and the costs of recruiting and training replacement staff. A business which does not implement safe measures in the workplace could face expensive legal costs and negative media coverage, which will impact on their reputation.

Health and safety issues when using office equipment

Studied ☐

The use of office equipment has been linked to shoulder, neck and back problems and eye strain. The likelihood of these issues occurring can be minimised by:

- a working area that allows users to move equipment so that they can work comfortably
- a workstation and equipment that can be adjusted to users' individual needs
- lighting which is bright and well positioned to avoid eye strain
- users having knowledge of correct seating position and posture and avoiding sitting in the same position for long periods
- a computer monitor which is adjustable for the user's height and positioned at an appropriate distance for the user. The monitor should have a screen size suitable for its intended use and have adjustable brightness and contrast controls.
- a chair which is height adjustable and allows the user to be positioned at the right height for the screen and keyboard
- a keyboard which is tilt adjustable
- a mouse or other pointing device which is positioned close by so the user can use it with a relaxed arm and a straight wrist
- if relevant, a foot rest for users who are unable to rest their feet flat on the floor.

Figure 2.3 Office equipment, such as a tilt adjustable keyboard, can help prevent shoulder, neck and back problems

Health and safety legislation

All employees who use office equipment should be aware of the relevant health and safety legislation for working safely.

- **Health and Safety at Work Act 1974** – the main UK legislation for health and safety in the workplace. It highlights the importance of providing a safe and secure working environment and the need to provide employees with training.
- **Workplace (Health, Safety and Welfare) Regulations 1992** – focuses on making sure that the working environment is safe. The legislation makes reference to workstations and seating and the maintenance of equipment.
- **The Health and Safety (Display Screen Equipment) Regulations 1992** – focuses on the employer risk assessing workstations to prevent injuries and health problems.

Safe lifting techniques

Lifting or carrying large items (stationery to refill the printer, documents for meetings, or large boxes) is the cause of many work-related accidents or injuries, including back problems. The workplace should be **risk assessed** and the business should implement ways to reduce unnecessary lifting and moving of large items. This could include having paper delivered to the print room and stored at waist height and providing trolleys to move large, bulky boxes.

Employees should be trained on safe lifting techniques for lifting and carrying large or bulky items correctly. Safe lifting techniques should include:

- Identifying if the object can be easily moved – try to tilt or push the object first. Always ask for help with heavy, large or bulky objects. Check for handles; if nothing is available a belt or straps should be used.
- Making sure the route is clear and straightforward – avoid stairs if possible and use lifts; remove any obstacles in the way and check that the unloading area is clear.
- Lifting the item safely – face the object with legs shoulder-width apart; bend the legs, let the legs and not the back do the work; grip the item firmly with both hands; keep the item close to the body and carefully push up with the legs.
- Lifting from high places – never reach up, always use a ladder; slide the object slowly towards the edge of the shelf and take firm grip of the object before moving down the ladder.
- Moving the item – take small steps and move slowly and carefully.

- Unloading – always face the area where the object is to be placed and lower the object slowly, bending knees and not the back; keep fingers out of the way. If placing on a shelf, put the object on the edge and slide slowly into position.

Figure 2.4 Adopting safe lifting techniques can help to avoid injuries

Following instructions

Studied ☐

Manufacturer's manuals will help equipment users to use equipment correctly and to prevent any health or safety issues. Training on new equipment and training manuals should provide guidance on the safe use of all pieces of office equipment.

✓

Topic B.2 Knowledge recap questions

1. Which legislation was introduced to protect employees who work regularly on computers?

2. Why is it important to use proper techniques for lifting and moving heavy objects?

3. What is meant by the term 'risk assessment'?

Assessment guidance for learning aim B

- -

2B.P2 **Describe the use of office equipment to meet different business requirements**

- -

✍ Learner answer

The office equipment I am using is:

- the telephone
- the computer
- printer
- photocopier
- work desk and chair.

Assessor report: The command verb for 2B.P2 is **describe**; to achieve this the learner will need to give a clear description of how office equipment is used to meet different business requirements – think of it as 'painting a picture with words'. The learner has set the scene by listing the office equipment they will describe.

✍ Learner answer

The telephone is used to provide information to and get information from customers, suppliers and other businesses. A business can use the telephone to talk to accountants, lawyers or the tax office. AT Engineering provides the fitters with mobile phones so that they can stay in contact with managers and the administrator when they are working off site. The Rink has a telephone system that allows the administrator to put forward calls to other people. The businesses have voicemail so callers can leave messages when no one is available. This is important for AT Engineering because it may be calls from customers who need work doing.

The computer can be used for lots of different tasks. Staff at AT Engineering use computers to produce Word documents such as letters, invoices and reports. They also use Excel to produce spreadsheets on sales and profits and financial reports.

Staff at The Rink use the computer for similar documents but they also produce their marketing posters on the computer. Both AT Engineering and The Rink use the computer to type up the agenda and minutes from meetings. Email is used to inform staff about the meetings and it is easy to attach copies of the agenda, minutes and any other documents to the email. Both businesses can use the internet to find information and to keep in contact with customers or suppliers by email. Both AT Engineering and The Rink have websites which provide information on what they do and contact details. Customers can have access to this information 24/7.

Assessor report: The learner has made a good start at describing the use of office equipment and is using examples from the two businesses used in 2A.P1 to help describe how office equipment meets business requirements.

Learner answer

The printer is used to make hard copies of any document produced by the computer. The hard copies can be sent to customers or suppliers or the business may want to keep a copy in a manual file. AT Engineering has paper files for all customers and suppliers and copies of the printed invoices are placed in the files. The Rink prints coloured copies of their posters and advertisements which are placed in the reception area so customers know about the events.

Assessor report: The learner has continued to describe the office equipment they have listed and now just needs to produce evidence for the work desk, photocopier and office chair.

Assessor report – overall

Is the evidence sufficient to satisfy the grading criterion?

The learner has produced a relevant list of the office equipment and has developed this further by describing how some pieces of equipment are used to meet different business requirements. To achieve 2B.P2 the learner will need to provide evidence on the work desk, photocopier and office chair.

What additional evidence, if any, is required?

To achieve 2B.P2 the learner will need to describe how the work desk, office chair and the photocopier meet different business requirements.

2B.P3 Demonstrate using office equipment safely, in accordance with health and safety legislation

✎ Learner answer

I have used my work placement at The Rink for 2B.P3. The office equipment I am going to demonstrate is: the computer, the printer, the photocopier, my office chair and the telephone.

My line manager at The Rink completed the observation statements.

Assessor report: The command verb for 2B.P3 is **demonstrate**, which is to provide several examples or related evidence which clearly shows how you have used office equipment safely and in accordance with health and safety legislation.

The learner has clearly identified the equipment to be used for the observation. The minimum requirement for 2B.P3 is a computer, printer, telephone and office chair. The learner has selected more than sufficient equipment to satisfy the requirements of the grading criterion.

✎ Learner answer

I have attached the observation document from my line manager.

Learner name:	Jack Brown
Assessor name:	Tom Press
Qualification:	Edexcel BTEC Level 2 First Award in Business
Unit:	Unit 7: Providing business support
Description of activity and grading criterion	
2B.P3 – Demonstrate using office equipment safely, in accordance with health and safety legislation	
Jack is working in an administration job role at The Rink and was observed demonstrating how to work safely on the computer, printer and photocopier.	
What the learner did	
Jack used the computer to produce an invoice and a letter for a school that used the pool. Jack printed one copy of each document. Jack photocopied the papers for the team meeting.	

How the learner met the requirements of the grading criterion

11\09\2012 – Jack adopted the correct posture (a) and moved the keyboard so that it was in the correct position for him to use (b). Jack adjusted the screen so that it was at the right height (c) and then logged on to the computer using the correct login and password. Although the document was clearly visible Jack demonstrated how he could adjust the brightness and contrast of the screen (d). The letter and invoice were produced using the house style. When asked about health and safety when working on the computer Jack responded correctly by identifying the need to take regular breaks and to have the font large enough to see easily (e).

Jack switched on the printer and checked that there was sufficient paper. Jack brought up the printer tab to check there was sufficient ink and printed one copy of each document. Jack demonstrated how he would change the ink cartridge and how a paper jam could be removed. Jack pointed out the instruction poster for replacing ink cartridges, paper and how to remove paper jams. Jack knew which technician to contact if he could not resolve any problems with the computer or printer (f).

Jack switched on the photocopier and waited patiently for it to go through the setting up sequence. While waiting Jack pointed out the poster which provides clear information on how to use the photocopier and how to resolve problems. Jack filled the paper tray and chose the right number of copies then back to back copying. Jack demonstrated how to find a jam and how it could be removed. Jack knew which technician to contact if he could not resolve any problems.

When asked, Jack knew that old ink cartridges were not placed with paper waste and indicated the boxes for storing old cartridges (e). All pieces of equipment were used efficiently and safely.

Learner signature: Jack Brown	**Date:** 11/09/2012
Assessor signature: Tom Press	**Date:** 11/09/2012

Assessor report: The assessor has produced a detailed personalised observation statement which clearly demonstrates how the learner used the computer safely (for example, adopting correct posture **a**, positioning the keyboard correctly **b** and adjusting screen height **c**, contrast and brightness **d**). The assessor has clearly identified when additional questions have been asked and has correctly recorded the learner response **e**. The observation also includes a demonstration of safe use of the printer **f**. The observation is signed and dated by both the learner and the assessor.

Assessor report – overall

Is the evidence sufficient to satisfy the grading criterion?

The learner has clearly and concisely identified the equipment that they were to use for the demonstration. The assessor has produced a good observation document but it only covers two pieces of equipment (the computer and printer) and would not be sufficient to satisfy the minimum requirement highlighted in the unit specification. The observation statement provided for 2B.P3 could be supported by annotated photographs.

What additional evidence, if any, is required?

To achieve 2B.P3 the assessor would need to observe the learner demonstrating safe use of the telephone and an office chair.

2B.M1 Explain the appropriate uses of office equipment types, features and functions to suit different business purposes

✍ Learner answer

> The office equipment I am using for 2B.M1 is the telephone, computer, printer, photocopier, work desk and chair.

Assessor report: The command verb for 2B.M1 is explain and to achieve this the learner will need to set out in detail, with reasons, the appropriate use of office equipment types, features and functions to suit different business purposes. This is more difficult than describing or listing, so it can help to give an example to show what you mean. Start by introducing the topic then give the 'how' or 'why'.

The learner has correctly listed the office equipment they will use to provide evidence for 2B.M1.

✍ Learner answer

> The telephone is an effective method of communicating with colleagues internally and for talking to customers, suppliers and other external organisations. Employees are trained on how to make and respond to telephone calls so that they are polite and present a good image for the business. Most businesses, to ensure consistency, will have set procedures for making calls and answering the phone. Most telephones have voicemail so if no one is available the customer can still leave a message. A telephone system, like the one at The Rink, can transfer calls from department to department, hold a call and play advertisements for future events when callers are on hold. Mobile phones mean that employees can keep in contact with colleagues, customers or suppliers when they are out of the office or in a different country.

Assessor report: The learner has made a good start by explaining the features and functions of the telephone for different business purposes and now needs to continue to do the same for the computer, printer, photocopier, workstation and chair.

✍ Learner answer

The computer is one of the most important and useful pieces of office equipment. Documents produced on the computer will look smart and professional and create a good image of the business. The business can use the computer to design templates for all documents which display the business logo, the business slogan or objective. The business could use the computer to produce a cash flow forecast, which will help plan how they will use resources, or to produce sales and profit forecasts for meetings. Financial documents can be produced for tax purposes, to get a loan and for the end of the year financial records. The Excel documents can be made into charts and graphs which can be used, for example, to show how sales or profits have gone up or down. The managers could use slideshow presentations to show how the business is doing, and The Rink uses PowerPoint presentations to show customers about the facilities and future events. Lots of businesses, like The Rink, will use the computer to design professional looking promotional posters or leaflets, which can be displayed or sent out to customers. The documentation for external meetings could be made to look professional with the business logo and clear fonts and this will create a good image for the business and impress other businesses.

Assessor report: The learner has explained the feature and functions of the computer and has given examples to explain how a business will use the different functions. They have not yet explained the features and functions of the printer, photocopier, desk and chair.

Assessor report – overall

Is the evidence sufficient to satisfy the grading criterion?

The learner has produced some good work so far for 2B.M1 and has used examples to help explain how the different features and functions of the office equipment are used. The learner will need to continue this and provide evidence for the printer, photocopier, workstation and chair.

What additional evidence, if any, is required?

To achieve 2B.M1 the learner will need to explain how the features and functions of the photocopier, printer, workstation and chair meet different business purposes.

2B.M2 Demonstrate understanding of the application of safe lifting techniques when using office equipment

✎ Learner answer

I have used my work placement at The Rink to provide the evidence for 2B.M2. I have produced a poster on safe lifting techniques and my line manager will submit a witness statement on how I lifted and moved the boxes of printing paper.

Assessor report: The command verb for 2B.M2 is **demonstrate**, which is to provide several examples or related evidence which clearly support that the leaner has an understanding of the application of safe lifting techniques. This may include showing practical skills.

The learner has clearly identified how the evidence for 2B.M2 will be generated.

✎ Learner answer

A GUIDE FOR LIFTING AND CARRYING ITEMS SAFELY
which will prevent back, shoulder and neck injuries

- Look and check how heavy the box or item is before trying to move it
- Tilt the item to see if can be moved easily or if you will need help
- Decide whether there is anything available to hold or whether you will need to add handles
- Make sure there is sufficient room to lift the item and there are no obstacles in your way
- Check that the route is clear
- If it is a tall item ask someone to help guide you
- If the item is on the ground – stand facing the item with feet apart
- Keep your back straight, bend with your legs to reach the item
- Keep the item close to your body and begin to stand slowly and lift
- Take small steps
- To put the item down, keep your back straight and bend your legs
- If you feel uncomfortable – STOP and put the item down
- If the item is above you, use a ladder
- If the item is too heavy ask for help or get a trolley from the front office

Assessor report: The poster does highlight that the learner is aware of the need to use safe lifting techniques but the command verb for 2B.M2 is to **demonstrate**, so the learner will need to demonstrate how to lift items safely.

✍ Learner answer

I have attached the observation document from my line manager.

Learner name:	Jack Brown
Assessor name:	Tom Press
Qualification:	Edexcel BTEC Level 2 First Award in Business
Unit:	Unit 7: Providing business support

Description of activity and grading criterion

2B.M2 Demonstrate understanding of the application of safe lifting techniques when using office equipment

Jack is working in an administration job role at The Rink and was observed demonstrating how to lift and move boxes of materials from the office to the meeting room.

What the learner did

Jack had photocopied documents which were required for a team meeting. Jack was asked to box up the documents and to take the boxes from the office to the meeting room.

How the learner met the requirements of the grading criterion

13\09\2012 – Jack had packed the documents into three boxes and before starting to move the boxes checked that they were not too heavy to lift and move **(a)**. Jack checked that the boxes were sealed correctly and that he could hold on to the bottom of each box without them splitting open **(a)**.

Jack checked that the relevant doors were open and that there were no obstacles in the route or in the meeting room **(a)**. Jack asked a colleague to make sure that no one closed the meeting room door **(a)**.

Jack stood facing the box and lifted with his back straight and knees bent. The box was held close to his chest and he used his legs to push into the standing position **(a)**. Jack walked slowly and carefully along the corridor to the meeting room, where he placed the edge of the box on the table and slide the box towards the centre **(a)**. Jack followed the same procedure for each box.

When asked why it was important to use safe lifting techniques Jack explained that it was to prevent injuries to the back, neck and shoulder **(b)**. Jack also commented that employees would need training to lift heavy items and this could prevent them from being off sick with injuries or back problems **(b)**. Jack said that for very heavy objects he would ask for help and use the trolley from the front office **(b)**.

A good effort, well done Jack.

Learner signature: Jack Brown	Date: 13/09/2012
Assessor signature: Tom Press	Date: 13/09/2012

Assessor report: The assessor has produced a detailed observation statement, which is correctly personalised and clearly demonstrates how the learner used correct lifting techniques **a**. The assessor has clearly identified when additional questions have been asked and has correctly recorded the learner response **b**. The observation is signed and dated by both the learner and the assessor.

Assessor report – overall

Is the evidence sufficient to satisfy the grading criterion?

The learner has produced an informative poster on the application of safe lifting techniques and has been observed demonstrating safe lifting techniques during their work placement. The assessor has produced a good observation document which provides clear evidence on how the learner demonstrated safe lifting techniques and responded to questions. The observation statement and poster provided for 2B.M2 could be supported by annotated photographs.

What additional evidence, if any, is required?

The evidence submitted is sufficient to satisfy the grading criterion for 2B.M2.

2B.D1 Analyse the contribution that office equipment makes to the provision of business support

✍ Learner answer

The two examples I am going to use for 2B.D1 are the business meeting I arranged for The Rink and research from my placement at AT Engineering.

Assessor report: The command verb for 2B.D1 is **analyse** and to achieve this the learner will need to identify separate pieces of office equipment and say how each one contributes to business support provision.

The learner has satisfied the requirement of the unit assessment guidance by identifying that the initial evidence will come from their own experience of supporting a meeting and the second analysis from research.

✍ Learner answer

For the meeting at The Rink I used several pieces of office equipment including a computer and printer, a photocopier, a laptop with projector, a workstation and chair and a telephone.

My workstation is in the large administration office and is near the window, with plenty of desk space for documents, a computer and a phone. The printer is on a separate desk by the door so that it can be used by all staff and the photocopier is located in a small room near the main administration office. The chair back and height have been adjusted so that I am comfortable when working at my desk. I have also adjusted the height and distance for my computer screen.

Assessor report: The learner has started to set the scene but has currently only highlighted how the workstation and chair satisfy legislation. The learner will need to analyse how the computer contributed to the business support provision for the meeting.

I have sat at a workstation to produce most of the documents for the meeting and it is important that I am comfortable and working safely. I used the computer software to produce the agenda for the meeting and I saved it in a file so that I could email it to all the staff. The format of the agenda, with the business logo, was already set up in a saved file on the computer so I only had to change the date and the agenda items, which saved me time. Because I used the computer to produce the documents I could use the spell and grammar check and the presentation was more neat and professional than if I had done it by hand. I used the email package on the computer to send the agenda and copies of the minutes from the last meeting to all staff. I only had to type one email because I could select the 'all staff' group from the email contact list and attach copies of the agenda and the minutes. I could use the spell check to check that the email was okay to send, and because I have a copy of the email in the sent box I have proof of when and to whom I sent the email. If I did not have access to email I would have had to write a memo and then photocopy the agenda and minutes, put them in envelopes, and then put them in the internal mail for all staff. The email process is much quicker and the staff could have access to the email and documents within minutes.

I was also able to use the computer to type up the minutes for the meeting and, as for the agenda, there is already a template set up so I just needed to add the information. I used the spell and grammar check before I sent the draft copy to Mr Thomas by email for checking. When Mr Thomas sent an email to say the minutes were okay I emailed a copy to all staff. The email process saved time, as I did not have to wait to see Mr Thomas for the minutes to be checked and I did not have to photocopy the minutes and put them in the internal post for all staff.

I printed one copy of each document so that I would have spare copies for the meeting. I could select to print one copy of each document and to save paper I selected back to back copies for the minutes. The printer can print in just black or colour, the colour print makes the business logo stand out. I could print more than one copy of each document but the office procedure is to use the photocopier for more than three copies. If I did not have access to the printer or photocopier I would have to produce copies of the same document by hand which would take time and would not look as neat.

I used the photocopier to produce hard copies of the sales figures and spare copies of the last minutes and agenda. I used the collation and staple option on the photocopier and this saved me from having to put the documents in order and then stapling them.

I used the phone to contact some staff to confirm their attendance at the meeting. When staff were not available I was able to leave a message on the voicemail for them. This meant I did not to run around the centre looking for them.

Assessor report: The learner has made a good analysis on how the workstation, chair and computer used at The Rink contributed to the business support process for the meeting. The learner has started by describing what they did and goes on to analyse how this contributed to the workplace. The learner has not yet analysed the contribution of the photocopier, laptop and projector, printer and the phone and should do so here. They also now need to provide a second analysis, based on research, on the contribution that office equipment makes to the provision of business support.

Assessor report – overall

Is the evidence sufficient to satisfy the grading criterion?

The learner has produced a good analysis on how the equipment used contributed to the business support process for the meeting at The Rink. The unit assessment guidance clearly states that the learner needs to provide two examples for 2B.D1: one from their own experience of supporting a meeting and one from research. The learner needs to produce the work for the second example, from research. The learner could use media and internet research or research at businesses they know well.

What additional evidence, if any, is required?

The learner will need to produce evidence of their research on the contribution that office equipment makes to the business support provision.

Learning aim C

Organise and provide support for meetings

Learning aim C provides an introduction to the different types of meetings and all the activities and documentation required to make a meeting run smoothly and efficiently.

Assessment criteria

2C.P4	Organise a meeting according to specified requirements using a checklist.
2C.P5	Produce accurate documents required prior to a meeting and take notes during the meeting.
2C.P6	Provide all required support for a meeting, including follow-up activities.
2C.M3	Explain the organisation and support required for different types of meetings.
2C.M4	Produce accurate and detailed post-meeting documentation (including minutes) prepared from notes taken during meeting discussions.
2C.D2	Evaluate own contribution to providing support before, during and after the meeting, and suggest improvements.

Topic C.1 Types of meeting

Meeting size

Studied ☐

Meetings will vary in size from a small informal discussion between colleagues in the office, to a formal annual general meeting where a large number of shareholders are likely to attend.

Internal and external meetings

Studied ☐

A meeting can be an internal meeting with work colleagues and managers to discuss items such as sales or profits figures and changes to business structure or procedures. An external meeting will be held with agencies or suppliers from outside the business and could be to discuss issues such as the quality and pricing of raw materials.

Formal and informal meetings

Studied ☐

An informal meeting will take less time to arrange and manage and may require fewer resources than a more formal meeting. An informal meeting usually has a more relaxed atmosphere than a formal meeting – some will have a set agenda and others will be impromptu, unplanned meetings with no formal agenda. An informal meeting could be a discussion between workplace colleagues on sales or plans to arrange a social event.

A formal meeting is a planned meeting with a set agenda and objectives. Annual General Meetings (AGMs) and board meetings are examples of formal meetings. All public companies and any private companies which trade their shares are required to hold an AGM to provide shareholders with an update on business activities and the future plans.

Figure 3.1

Confidential meetings

Studied ☐

These are held to discuss an employee's problem, issue or concern; human resources issues; or sensitive trading negotiations. When a confidential item is on the agenda any delegates who are not required to be present will be asked to leave the meeting. A record of this discussion is recorded on a separate document and the information is not included in the minutes of the meeting circulated to delegates.

Team meetings

Studied ☐

These meetings keep team members informed on any updates and allow any issues or problems to be discussed. To be effective and to encourage motivation, a comfortable environment should be provided in which employees are encouraged to voice their opinions and to put forward their ideas and suggestions.

Topic C.1 Knowledge recap questions

1. What information would not be recorded in the minutes of a meeting?

2. Why would a manager use a meeting to inform employees about any planned changes?

Topic C.2 Organising meetings

Meetings can be arranged for many different reasons (for example, to share information, solve problems, generate new ideas and look at ways to increase efficiency). To be effective it is important that people attending know the purpose and objectives of the meeting.

Meeting brief and agenda

Studied ☐

It is important to clarify the meeting brief (the purpose of the meeting), who is required to attend, the equipment requirements and who will be responsible for providing any support requirements.

Documentation provided for the meeting should look professional, provide accurate information and be formatted in the house style.

The agenda should clearly highlight the venue, date and time of the meeting, the purpose of the meeting and the items for discussion. The agenda should be circulated to allow sufficient time for people to prepare and to collect any relevant information or resources.

Checking dates and confirming budget

Studied ☐

If it is essential that certain people attend the meeting it may be beneficial to check their availability before setting the date and meeting time. Always confirm the budget that is available for the meeting before booking any venue or ordering any resources.

Choosing and booking venues

Studied ☐

When booking and choosing the venue it is important to consider the number of people who will be attending the meeting. The venue should have sufficient toilet facilities and be easily accessible for all delegates, including any delegate with special requirements. If people are travelling from different areas it should be in a central location with easy access to public transport and sufficient car parking.

Figure 3.2 It is important to book a suitable venue for a meeting

UNIT 7 Providing Business Support

Sending meeting invitations

The invitation to attend the meeting should clearly highlight the purpose of the meeting, the venue and the date and time of the meeting. The invitation should include the meeting agenda, any relevant reading materials and a copy of the minutes from the previous meeting. Everyone who is required to attend should be given plenty of notice and sufficient time to prepare. It is a good idea to ask delegates to confirm their attendance in advance.

Arranging catering, equipment and resources

Equipment and resources should be booked well in advance of the meeting. The speakers may require computers, overhead projectors, flip charts and pens or display stands.

The catering arrangements should be booked and information obtained on meals for people with special dietary requirements.

Venue details and transport information

Delegates will need information on how to get to the venue. They should be provided with a map to the venue and the address, including the postcode for use in car navigation systems. Details on public transport and local hotels are also useful, so that delegates can select the most convenient and cost effective way to reach the venue.

Recording attendance and apologies

A record should be kept and regularly updated on the delegates who have confirmed their attendance at the meeting and those who have sent their apologies.

Identifying special requirements

All delegates should be asked in advance whether they have any special requirements. This could include needing wheelchair access to the venue or having special dietary requirements – this information should be forwarded to the staff at the venue well in advance of the meeting.

Topic C.2 Knowledge recap questions

1. List three responsibilities of the employee who is organising and planning a meeting.

2. Why is it important to know what budget is available?

3. What information would delegates need before the meeting?

Topic C.3 Supporting meetings

To ensure that the meeting runs smoothly there are several tasks and activities that need to be organised.

Documentation for attendees

Studied ☐

On the day of the meeting additional copies of the agenda, reading material sent out with the agenda and the minutes of the last meeting should be available for delegates who have forgotten to bring their copies.

Attendance list and apologies

Studied ☐

An attendance list should be available to tick off the delegates who attended the meeting.

After the meeting, an accurate list should be made of the delegates who attended the meeting and those who did not. The list should also identify the delegates who sent apologies.

Checking room and equipment

Studied ☐

The room should be checked to ensure that the layout is appropriate and that there are sufficient tables and chairs. All booked equipment should be in place and any additional materials should be close at hand.

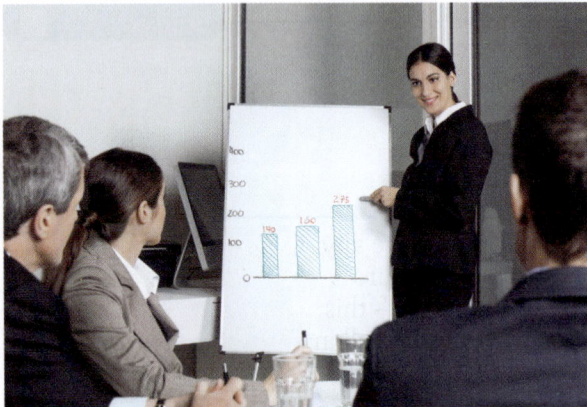

Figure 3.3 It is important to check that any equipment required has been set up

Equipment should be switched on and tested. Any software or electronic documents should be opened and checked and any required passwords or logging-in information should be available for speakers.

Health and safety and refreshments

Studied ☐

Delegates should be informed about health and safety issues, fire exits and any planned fire drills and be told where to find refreshments and facilities such as toilets.

Minutes

Studied ☐

It should be clearly recorded if the minutes from the last meeting were accurate. The chairperson could ask for any updates on actions from the last meeting.

The minutes are an accurate record of what was discussed, the decisions that were made and any agreed actions. They do not have to be a word-by-word account of what was said but they must be clear and accurate. The minutes should also record the date, time and location of the meeting, who attended, who sent apologies and the date and time of the next meeting.

✔

Topic C.3 Knowledge recap questions

1. What documentation should an employee supporting a meeting have available on the day?

2. List four responsibilities on the day of the meeting of the employee who is responsible for organising the meeting.

3. What are 'minutes of a meeting'?

Topic C.4 Follow-up activities

There are several activities that must be completed at the end of and following a meeting.

Clearing the venue

Studied ☐

When all the delegates have left, the meeting room must be left clean and tidy. All crockery and cutlery must be placed on the refreshment table or trolley and either left for collection or returned to the kitchen. Tables and chairs must be returned to their original positions. All spare confidential documents must be destroyed and all other resources taken back to the office. All equipment should be switched off.

Writing up minutes

Studied ☐

Minutes should be produced as soon as possible after the meeting and distributed within the agreed timescale. They should be an accurate record of the main points of the discussion, the decisions made and any agreed actions. The purpose of the meeting, the venue and the date and time of the meeting should all be recorded on the minutes. They should be written in the correct format or house style with no spelling or grammatical errors and checked for accuracy by the person who chaired the meeting before they are distributed.

Circulating documents

Studied ☐

The minutes should be circulated with any other relevant documents to all delegates including those who sent apologies and did not attend.

Monitoring completion of agreed actions

Studied ☐

Any identified actions should be monitored and any progress made should be recorded for discussion at the next meeting.

Topic C.4 Knowledge recap questions

✓

1. List three responsibilities at the end of the meeting of the employee responsible for organising the meeting.

2. Why is it important to get the minutes checked and authorised before they are distributed to delegates?

3. Why is it important to monitor agreed actions?

Assessment guidance for learning aim C

2A.P4 **Organise a meeting according to specified requirements using a checklist**

✍ Learner answer

I have been asked to make the plans for the monthly meeting for all employees (including managers and trainers) at The Rink. The meeting is to update employees on current changes, to discuss any issues, to discuss the rise or fall in sales and to discuss the arrangements for the special events in the following month.

Assessor report: The command verb for 2C.P4 is **organise** and to achieve this the learner will need to make the arrangements for a meeting.

The learner has set the scene by identifying the purpose of the meeting and will need to produce a checklist of all the relevant tasks and activities.

✍ Learner answer

I have decided to divide my checklist into three sections: things to do before the meeting; things to do on the day of the meeting and during the meeting; and things to do after the meeting.

This is my checklist:

Section 1 – tasks for before the meeting	
Task	**Tick and date when completed**
Ask for location, date and time Ask for agenda items and how much is available for refreshments	
Prepare agenda	
Book the room – make sure it is recorded in the diary	
Book refreshments – check what is available	
Photocopy the resources	

Book laptop and projector – send email to technician to set it up	
Prepare a list of who should be attending	
Section 2 – tasks for day of meeting and during the meeting	
Check room layout – tables and chairs	
Check equipment is in room and ask technician to check it is working	
Take spare resources to room	
Welcome people to the meeting	
Set out and serve refreshments	
Make notes during the meeting	
Section 3 – tasks following the meeting	
Collect in spare documents and shred them	
Collect in cups, plates and cutlery ready for collection by the kitchen staff	
Tidy chairs and tables	
Ask technician to disconnect the laptop and projector and return them to the office	
Write up minutes	
Get minutes checked	
Send out minutes and any other information to all staff	

Assessor report: The learner has listed several of the important tasks in the checklist but there are some important tasks that have been omitted. The learner has forgotten to add activities such as sending the agenda to all employees before the meeting and informing employees about the arrangements for the meeting; requesting information on special requirements; and producing a list of who attended the meeting and employees who sent apologies.

Assessor report – overall

Is the evidence sufficient to satisfy the grading criterion?

The learner has clearly highlighted that they are aware of tasks which must be completed before, during and after a meeting but the checklist does not fully list all the activities which need to be completed.

What additional evidence, if any, is required?

The learner would need to add the remaining activities to the checklist before 2C.P4 can be awarded.

Produce accurate documents required prior to a meeting and take notes during the meeting

✍ Learner answer

I have produced the following documents for the meeting:

- emails telling staff about the meeting and to book the room, equipment and refreshments
- a list to record employees who attended and any apologies
- the agenda
- my notes from the meeting signed by my line manager.

Assessor report: The command verb is **produce** and to achieve 2C.P5 the learner will need to create all the documents required prior to the meeting and submit the notes they made during the meeting.

The learner has set the scene by listing the documents they will need to produce prior to the meeting.

✍ Learner answer

These are screenshots of my emails.

	To...	All Staff
Send	Cc...	
	Bcc...	
	Subject	Monthly meeting
	📎	📄 Agenda.docx (14.8 KB)

Hello,
The monthly meeting for all staff is on Friday September 7th at 8:00 in the boardroom. The agenda is attached and breakfast will be provided. The meeting will last for approximately two hours and the centre will open promptly to customers at 10:30.

Regards,
Jack

	To...	Mr Jones
Send	Cc...	
	Bcc...	
	Subject	Room and equipment booking

Dear Mr Jones

Can you please book the board room for Friday September 7th from 8:00 to 10:30. The meeting is planned to last just two hours but Mr Thomas would like the extra 30 minutes. Could you please arrange for a laptop and projector to be in the room and ask the technician to check it on the morning of the meeting.

Thank you

Regards
Jack

	To...	Mrs Kelly
Send	Cc...	
	Bcc...	
	Subject	Refreshments

Dear Mrs Kelly

Can I please book breakfast for 20 members of staff in the board room on Friday September 7th at 8:00. Can you please arrange tea, coffee, fruit juice, a selection of sandwiches, pastries, fruit and biscuits. Can you please arrange for this to be invoiced to Mr Thomas

Thank you

Regards
Jack

Assessor report: The learner has submitted screenshots of the emails which contain sufficient information about the planned meeting. The first email shows that the learner attached a copy of the agenda for all staff.

These are copies of the agenda and the notes I made during the meeting. I have also included a copy of the completed meeting attendance log sheet (I prepared the blank meeting attendance record in advance of the meeting).

**Monthly meeting for all employees
Agenda**

THE RINK

1. Apologies

2. Minutes of the last meeting – action update

3. Changes to the reception area

4. Changing room procedures

5. Monthly sales and profits

6. Any other business

7. Date and time for next meeting

My notes from the meeting:

Notes from the meeting

1. *Apologies were received from W. Lime and F. Jones.*

2. *The minutes from the last meeting were accepted and agreed. Update K. Frey – new computer system was installed and is fully working.*

3. *Info T. Thomas The reception area – longer opening hours; no longer responsible for sorting and distributing mail; will sign for special deliveries etc.*

4. *Info T. Thomas complaints about dirty floors and rubbish - more bins, more inspections, inspection form to be signed, time - T. Press to monitor*

5. *H. Hall info on sales and profits – last year; this year better; last month; this month better*

6. *Reception staff asked about staff uniforms –when? T. Thomas – next week*

7. *12/10 at 8:00 – all staff*

Signed by

T Thomas

My completed attendance log – signed by staff who came to the meeting:

Meeting attendance log		
Date of meeting: 7th September 2012 Type of meeting: Monthly meeting – all staff		
Employee name	**Email and agenda sent**	**Employee signature**
T. Thomas	Yes	T. Thomas
K. Frey	Yes	K. Frey
H. Hall	Yes	H. Hall
W. Lime	Yes	
R. Kent	Yes	R. Kent
F. Jones	Yes	
P. Peters	Yes	P. Peters
T. Wise	Yes	T. Wise
J. Kite	Yes	J. Kite
T. Press	Yes	T. Press
J. Brown	Yes	J. Brown

Assessor report: The learner has submitted emails which show who was contacted to provide equipment and refreshments and a log sheet which shows that all employees were emailed about the meeting. The agenda does include some of the important details but does not show the date, time or location for the meeting. It would also be beneficial to record this information on the notes for the meeting.

Assessor report – overall

Is the evidence sufficient to satisfy the grading criterion?

The learner has provided clear evidence on who was contacted to provide support for the meeting and a clear log of which employees attended the meeting. The agenda provides employees with information about the content for the meeting but not where or when it is and this will need to be added before 2C.P5 can be awarded. The notes have been signed by a senior member of staff and should provide sufficient information for the learner to produce the minutes. It would be beneficial to record the location, date and time of the meeting on the notes.

What additional evidence, if any, is required?

For the learner to be awarded 2C.P5 the agenda and notes should be amended to show the location, date and time of the meeting.

✎ **Learner answer**

For 2C.P6 I have produced a list of what I did before, during and after the meeting. My line manager has submitted an observation statement on the tasks and activities I completed.

Assessor report: The command verb for 2C.P6 is **provide** and to achieve this the learner will need to generate evidence to show they provided all the required support for the meeting.

The learner has correctly identified how the evidence for 2C.P6 will be generated.

✎ **Learner answer**

Section 1 – before the meeting

My first task was to ask Mr Thomas, a senior manager, why the meeting was being held, the location, date and time. I also asked about the budget for the refreshments. I then sent three emails: a group email to inform staff about the meeting; one to book the room and equipment; and one to arrange the refreshments. I produced the agenda and photocopied the minutes from the last meeting. I added the names to the meeting attendance log and printed a copy. I put a tick against all the staff who had been sent the agenda. I phoned to check that the room, equipment and refreshments were booked and available.

Section 2 – on the day and during the meeting

I arrived early to move the tables and chairs into the correct positions. I asked the technician to check the laptop and projector; it was all working. I placed a copy of the minutes from the last meeting at each seat and then helped to lay out and serve the refreshments. I asked all staff to sign the log. When Mr Thomas started the meeting I made notes and asked him to sign them at the end of the meeting.

Section 3 – after the meeting

I typed up the minutes and sent them out to all staff. I made a task sheet for the actions and added information when tasks were completed.

Assessor report: Sections 1 and 2 provide a good list of the support provided by the learner but in Section 1 the learner has made no reference to sending the agenda to the employees prior to the meeting. Section 3 is very brief and makes no reference to tidying the room or getting the minutes checked before they were distributed. The evidence is currently not sufficient for the learner to be awarded 2C.P6.

✍ Learner answer

The observation statement by my line manager.

Learner name:	Jack Brown
Assessor name:	Tom Press
Qualification:	Edexcel BTEC Level 2 First Award in Business
Unit:	Unit 7: Providing Business Support

Description of activity and grading criterion

2C.P6 Provide all required support for a meeting, including follow-up activities

Jack is working in an administration job role at The Rink and was observed producing documents and providing support for the monthly meetings for all employees at The Rink.

What the learner did

Jack was asked to arrange and support the monthly meeting at The Rink. Jack was provided with all the relevant information about the meeting by Mr Thomas.

How the learner met the requirements of the grading criterion

Jack asked Mr Thomas for all the relevant information about the meeting and then sent clear emails to inform all employees. Jack booked the room, equipment and refreshments by email giving all the relevant information. Jack did confirm by telephone that the room, equipment and refreshments were booked for the right day and time.

Jack produced all the relevant documents such as the agenda, attendance log with all employees listed, the minutes and the log for actions. When possible Jack used the templates for the documents which are in the house style with The Rink logo. Everything was well organised and prepared for the meeting.

Jack set out the room and asked the technician to check the equipment. Jack welcomed the staff to the meeting and helped to serve the refreshments.

The meeting ran smoothly and Jack had produced extra copies of the minutes from the last meeting for employees who forgot to bring their copy. The notes made during the meeting were clear, concise and in sufficient detail from which to produce the minutes.

Learner signature: Jack Brown	Date: 10/09/2012
Assessor signature: Tom Press	Date: 10/09/2012

Assessor report: The observation statement does support the list generated by the learner about what they did before the meeting but has not provided any additional evidence on when the agenda was sent to the employees. There is no reference to the support during and after the meeting, including whether the room was left tidy and clean.

Assessor report – overall

Is the evidence sufficient to satisfy the grading criterion?

The learner has provided a clear list but some support activities have been omitted. The observation statement does identify the activities completed by Jack before the meeting but does not provide evidence on whether the agenda was sent out to employees well before the meeting so that they could be well prepared for the meeting. The observation statement does not provide any evidence on what Jack did during and after the meeting, including evidence on whether Jack tidied and cleared the room when the meeting had finished. It is important to make sure the room is left clean and tidy and that any documents are removed, especially if they contain confidential information.

Annotated photographs could be provided to support the work generated by the learner and the observation statement.

What additional evidence, if any, is required?

To achieve 2C.P6 the learner will need to add information to Section 3 of their list and the assessor will need to provide evidence that these activities were completed.

2C.M3 Explain the organisation and support required for different types of meetings

✍ Learner answer

There are a lot of tasks and activities involved in supporting meetings but the support required will depend on the type of meeting. Meetings will range from a small informal meeting for internal staff only to a large AGM for delegates who are both internal and external. All meetings require time to plan and organise tasks such as deciding who needs to attend and when and where to have the meeting, booking a venue, producing an agenda, getting equipment and refreshments and producing minutes.

Assessor report: The command verb for 2C.M3 is **explain** and to achieve this the learner will need to set out in detail the organisation and support required for different types of meetings. This is more difficult than describing or listing, so it can help to give an example to show what you mean.

The learner has set the scene by identifying that there are different types of meetings, all of which require organising and supporting in different ways.

✍ Learner answer

AT Engineering Ltd have lots of different types of meetings. They have:

- small internal meetings to discuss different jobs and what needs to be done
- staff meetings to discuss work or problems
- large meetings with external businesses to discuss repairs to existing machines. These meetings are held at locations around the country.
- meetings with external people such as lawyers or accountants
- yearly board meetings with the directors.

The Rink has lots of internal meetings and only a few external meetings. The meetings at The Rink are:

- internal meetings for different teams
- large internal monthly meetings for all staff
- meetings with external people such as lawyers or accountants
- external meetings with local council members.

AT Engineering's external meetings with other businesses are formal meetings and take longer to organise than internal meetings. A lot of the external meetings are with other businesses to discuss repairs, maintenance or the building of machines. These businesses are paying AT Engineering a lot of money to get their equipment fixed or updated so they will expect AT Engineering to be efficient in having all materials and information available for the meeting. The administrator will need to communicate with the managers at AT Engineering and the managers at the other business to find a convenient date, time and location. When the date is agreed the administrator will be responsible for finding a suitable venue, booking the room and organising refreshments. The venue, facilities and refreshments should present a good image for AT Engineering. Information on the location of the venue, the date and time of the meeting and directions to the venue are sent by email to the team at AT Engineering and managers at the other business. To keep arrangements clear and accurate the administrator is the main communication person for the team at AT Engineering, the other business and the venue.

The administrator will have responsibility for arranging laptops, samples of materials and any other relevant paperwork. AT Engineering staff take their own laptops to meetings because of the software packages they use.

The administrator will discuss the items for the agenda with managers at AT Engineering and will then produce an electronic copy which looks professional. The agenda and confirmation of the meeting are emailed to all relevant people so that they have time to prepare for the meeting. The administrator will communicate regularly with staff at the venue to make sure everything is planned and ready.

The administrator will arrive early to check that everything is organised and gives a good impression for the other business. The administrator will check the room layout, refreshments and laptop connections. After welcoming staff from the other business and helping to serve refreshments, the administrator is responsible for taking accurate notes on who attended and what decisions were made. The notes and the minutes could be used at a later date to provide evidence on what was agreed and discussed.

At the end of the meeting the administrator will collect any papers in, destroying any which are confidential, and will make sure that the room is looking tidy. The administrator's final task is to type up the minutes, get them confirmed and then distribute them to all relevant people. The actions are followed up by managers at AT Engineering and then feedback is given at the next meeting.

Assessor report: The learner has currently outlined the types of meetings held at both The Rink and AT Engineering and explained, in some detail, the organisation and support required for only one type of meeting (an external, formal meeting). The learner will need to provide evidence on other types of meetings, including informal meetings and internal meetings.

Assessor report – overall

Is the evidence sufficient to satisfy the grading criterion?

The learner has provided a clear list of the different types of meetings held at both AT Engineering and The Rink but has focused on explaining how formal, external meetings are organised and supported. The learner has provided some good evidence for formal meetings but should provide an explanation on the organisation and support required for an informal meeting. This will help confirm the learner's understanding and knowledge of the different types of meetings.

What additional evidence, if any, is required?

To achieve 2C.M3 the learner will need to explain the organisation and support required for internal and informal meetings.

Produce accurate and detailed post-meeting documentation (including minutes) prepared from notes taken during meeting discussions.

✎ Learner answer

For 2C.M4 I have produced
- the minutes for the meeting at The Rink
- the email to send out the minutes
- the action log sheet with updates.

Assessor report: The command verb is **produce** and to achieve 2C.M4 the learner will need to create detailed post-meeting documentation. The learner has clearly listed the types of post-meeting documentation that they will produce.

✎ Learner answer

The log sheet for actions from the meeting

Action log sheet		
Summary of action needed	Manager responsible	Date and record of any action taken
The intranet installed and all old files transferred	K. Frey	10/9 the intranet is fully operational and all files have now been updated
Changing room – check that inspections have been completed and that the log sheet is signed after every visit	T. Press	10/9 changing rooms are tidy and log sheet signed

17/9 changing rooms tidy, bins emptied and log sheets signed |
| Monitor the rink shop area | T. Press | 14/9 the same group of young people, mostly girls, have been making a nuisance of themselves in the shop and have been asked to move.

Have asked security to monitor the area and if the problem continues the group will not be allowed into the rink area. |

Assessor report: The learner has submitted an action log which highlights what action the member of staff responsible has implemented. It does not make reference to all the actions identified at the meeting. The learner should also have included a screenshot showing the email they sent to all staff, which included the minutes sent as an attachment.

✎ **Learner answer**

The minutes from the meeting.

Minutes
Monthly meeting Board room

● THE RINK ●

Present: T. Thomas, K. Frey, T. Press, J. Kite, F. Jones, H. Hall, R. Kent, P. Peters, T. Wise, J. Brown

Apologies: W. Lime, F. Jones

Minutes of the last meeting: The minutes from the last meeting were accepted as accurate and agreed by everyone. K. Frey provided the staff with an update on the new computer system. The new computer system and intranet are fully installed and working. The IT team are in the process of copying documents into files on the intranet and all policies and procedures should be added this week.

Changes to the reception area: T. Thomas outlined the changes for reception. The reception area would open for longer from 8:30–19:30. The reception staff were to wear their name badges and focus more on customer service. All mail would now go to the main office for sorting and delivering but the reception staff would still sign for any post requiring a signature. To remove the congestion when schools arrive, only staff are required to sign in but they must provide a list of all the pupils. A letter has been sent to the school and the feedback was positive to the new arrangements.

Changing room procedures: T. Thomas informed the meeting that there had been an increase in the number of complaints about the changing rooms. Most of the complaints concerned dirty floors and overflowing rubbish bins. T. Press said that more bins had been placed in the changing areas and that the cleaning log showed that the changing rooms had not been checked regularly. T. Press informed the cleaning team that they must complete the inspection at the set times and sign the inspection log. T. Thomas asked T. Press to monitor the process and to provide an update at the next meeting.

Monthly sales and profits: H. Hall's presentation showed that sales and profits had increased against last month's figures and the same time last year. T. Thomas asked for staff to email him with suggestions on how to improve the number of people using the gym.

Any other business: J. Kite from reception asked about the availability of new uniforms – T. Thomas informed the team they would be available next week. R. Kent said that there was same concerns about groups hanging around the rink shop at night and could there be more security. T. Thomas asked T. Press to ask security to monitor the situation and to provide feedback for the next meeting.

Date and time for next meeting: All staff on 12th October at 8:00

Assessor report: The learner has submitted detailed minutes from the meeting but the date and time of the meeting are not shown. There is also some confusion over the employees who attended the meeting: F. Jones is shown as sending apologies and attending the meeting. To achieve 2C.M4 the learner will need to correct the minutes of the meeting.

Assessor report – overall

Is the evidence sufficient to satisfy the grading criterion?

The learner has submitted a clear action log but it does not include all of the actions from the meeting. The minutes of the meeting are detailed and informative but the date and time are important and should be recorded on all meeting documentation. The minutes should be an accurate record of who was present during the meeting and the learner has shown F. Jones as sending apologies and attending. A screenshot of the email sending the minutes to all employees should have been included.

What additional evidence, if any, is required?

To achieve 2C.M4 the learner will need to add the time and date to the minutes and correctly list the employees who attended the meeting. They need to make sure all actions from the meeting are included in the action log and that a screenshot of the email sending the minutes to all employees is included.

Evaluate own contribution to providing support before, during and after the meeting, and suggest improvements

✍ Learner answer

My evaluation for 2C.D2 will focus on my strengths and weaknesses when preparing and organising the meeting at The Rink. There have been things that I have not done correctly and which I need to improve and I will make suggestions for these.

Assessor report: The command verb is **evaluate**, for which the learner will need to review the documentation they produced for the meeting and the contribution they made before, during and after the meeting and make suggestions for improvements.

The learner has correctly set the scene by explaining that their evaluation will focus on the strengths and weaknesses of the activities they completed for organising the meeting and the areas where improvements are needed.

✍ Learner answer

My strengths and weaknesses.

Strengths	Weaknesses
Before the meeting	
I found out all the relevant information about the time, date and purpose of the meeting.	
I used the template for the agenda and just changed the topics. The agenda had The Rink logo and there were no spelling errors. The email included all the information I missed on the agenda.	I did not put a date or time on the agenda and I did not show where the meeting was to be held. I did not know who had and had not read the agenda.
I photocopied the minutes from the last meeting and spare copies of the agenda.	I did not know how to change the settings on the photocopier and constantly asked for help.
I booked the room, equipment and refreshments and checked I after that they were booked. I knew who was to pay for the refreshments and sent this information in the email.	I told staff breakfast was to be provided but did not check for special dietary requirements.

On the day of the meeting	
I was at the room early to check everything was okay.	
I moved tables and chairs so that everyone could see the screen.	
I was well organised and everything looked neat and tidy when Mr Thomas arrived.	
I asked the technician to switch on and check the equipment and everything was working well.	
I helped set out the refreshments so that everything was easy to reach.	
I asked staff to sign the attendance sheet.	Not everyone signed the sheet – I am not sure whether Carl Wren was at the meeting.
I took notes on the main items.	My notes were not very detailed and I had to add bits from my memory and ask other staff for some information.
After the meeting	
The final minutes were good. I got Mr Thomas to check the minutes and sent them out quickly.	I forgot to add the date and time to the minutes. I had to check some of the information before I gave it to Mr Thomas. Some of the staff who were down as attending did not attend.
	The meeting room was not checked and documents were left in the meeting room.

Assessor report: The learner has produced an interesting table and has identified some strengths and weaknesses. The learner now needs to evaluate the points listed and make suggestions for improvements.

✍ Learner answer

I think that I was well organised for the meeting and that my documentation was one of my main weaknesses. I made sure all the information in the agenda was accurate so the staff knew what was to be discussed **a** but did forget to add other important information. The agenda did not show where the meeting was or the date and time **b**. This was the first time I have produced an agenda which was to be used at a real meeting so I should have got my line manager to check it. I forgot to include similar information on the minutes and I know this information is important for formal meetings. I have saved a copy of the agenda and minute templates to my files and highlighted in yellow the section which must be completed **c**.

I sent the agenda out by email and should have checked that the date was recorded as proof that the email was sent well before the meeting **b**.

I was nervous at the meeting and although I passed around the attendance sheet for signatures, some staff arrived late and I was not sure who was and who was not there. The email with the agenda did not ask for everyone to let me know if they could or could not attend and this could have prevented the confusion on who did and did not attend **b**. If staff had emailed I could have ticked them off on the attendance list and then focused more on staff who I had not heard from. During the meeting I could have also counted the staff and the signatures to see if they matched **c**.

The technician checked the laptop and projector so I knew that everything was okay. The email I sent with the agenda attachment did contain all the information that was missing from the agenda **a**.

I helped set out the table for the refreshments and served the hot drinks. The table was set out so that the staff could easily reach what they wanted. The breakfast did look tasty and I tried to keep the table tidy with bins available for tea bags and sugar wrappers **a**.

Assessor report: The learner has made a good start and has provided a good evaluation on some of the strengths **a** and weaknesses **b** identified in the table. The learner has also made clear suggestion on what improvements could be implemented to overcome the identified weaknesses **c**. The learner could include more information on the overall judgement of their performance.

✍ Learner answer

In my first email to staff about the meeting I should have asked about special dietary requirements for the breakfast. I do know that some staff are vegetarians and one is a diabetic but I am not sure whether there is anyone who has a wheat allergy **b**. The breakfast provided by the kitchen did include a good selection but I think I may have just been lucky this time. If I get the opportunity to organise other meetings I know I must ask about dietary and other special requirements in my first email. I have set up an email template which now includes all this information and where I just have to change the venue, date and time for the meeting **c**.

My notes for the meeting were not very detailed and I had to check some of the information with my line manager before I typed up the minutes for Mr Thomas to review. I had got most of the important points down but did not feel confident with what I had written **b**. Next time I would list the agenda items on my notepad before the meeting and just add the information in bullet points **c**.

Assessor report: The learner has continued to evaluate the points from the table and now needs to focus on how to overcome the weaknesses with photocopying skills and forgetting the importance of leaving the meeting room tidy and removing any documents.

Assessor report – overall

Is the evidence sufficient to satisfy the grading criterion?

The learner has submitted a good table which clearly highlights their strengths and weaknesses in planning and organising the meeting. The learner has developed some of the points from the table and evaluated how they contributed to providing support for the meeting. The learner has made clear suggestions on how the points identified so far can be improved. There are two points in the table which the learner has not provided evidence for: the photocopying and the activities at the end of the meeting when the room should be left clean and tidy.

What additional evidence, if any, is required?

To achieve 2C.D2 the learner will need to evaluate the strengths and weaknesses of their photocopying skills and make suggestions on how the photocopying weaknesses can be improved. The learner will also need to evaluate why the room was left untidy and suggest what should happen when organising future meetings. The learner should be encouraged to add some evidence on the overall judgement of their performance for planning and organising the meeting.

Sample assignment brief for learning aims A and B

PROGRAMME NAME:		BTEC Level 2 First Award in Business	
ASSESSOR:			
DATE ISSUED:		SUBMISSION DATE:	
INTERIM REVIEW:			

This assignment will assess the following learning aims and grading criteria:

A Understand the purpose of providing business support

B Use office equipment safely for different purposes.

2A.P1	Explain the purpose of different types of business support in two contrasting businesses.
2B.P2	Describe the use of office equipment to meet different business requirements.
2B.P3	Demonstrate using office equipment safely, in accordance with health and safety legislation.
2B.M1	Explain the appropriate uses of office equipment types, features and functions to suit different business purposes.
2B.M2	Demonstrate understanding of the application of safe lifting techniques when using office equipment.
2B.D1	Analyse the contribution that office equipment makes to the provision of business support.

Scenario

You are doing your work placement in the Student Information Centre where students come for advice on employment opportunities. A few of the learners on the business administration programme are interested in finding out more about the tasks involved in a business support position.

You have been asked to produce three informative leaflets which will provide the students with information on the different types of business support, the equipment they will need to use and guidance on working safely.

Task 1

Leaflet one will provide information on the business support role and the equipment used in the provision of business support.

Your leaflet will need to **explain** the purpose of different types of business support in two contrasting businesses.

Next, **describe** the use of office equipment to meet different business requirements.

Next, **explain** the appropriate uses of office equipment types, features and functions to suit different business purposes.

Finally, **analyse** the contribution that office equipment makes to the provision of business support.

Task 2

Leaflet two will provide guidance on how to use equipment safely.

Demonstrate using office equipment safely, in accordance with health and safety legislation. Your leaflet should include annotated photographs of you using **at least three pieces of equipment**.

Your teacher will produce an observation statement to support your evidence.

Task 3

Demonstrate understanding of the application of safe lifting techniques when using office equipment. Your leaflet should include annotated photographs of you demonstrating safe lifting techniques.

Your teacher will produce an observation statement to support your evidence.

Sample assignment brief for learning aim C

PROGRAMME NAME:		BTEC Level 2 First Award in Business
ASSESSOR:		
DATE ISSUED:		SUBMISSION DATE:
INTERIM REVIEW:		

This assignment will assess the following learning aim and grading criteria:

C Organise and provide support for meetings.

2C.P4 Organise a meeting according to specified requirements using a checklist.

2C.P5 Produce accurate documents required prior to a meeting and take notes during the meeting.

2C.P6 Provide all required support for a meeting, including follow-up activities.

2C.M3 Explain the organisation and support required for different types of meetings.

2C.M4 Produce accurate and detailed post-meeting documentation (including minutes) prepared from notes taken during meeting discussions.

2C.D2 Evaluate own contribution to providing support before, during and after the meeting, and suggest improvements.

Scenario

You have been asked by your line manager in the Student Office to organise and plan a meeting with local businesses to discuss work placements opportunities.

You will be responsible for planning and organising all of the activities before, during and after the meeting.

Task 1

Your first task is to identify the activities you will be responsible for and to produce a checklist. Your checklist will need to include the tasks and activities for before, during and after the meeting.

Task 2

Produce the documents required prior to a meeting, making sure they are clear and accurate.

You are also responsible for taking the notes during the meeting, which will be used for the minutes (remember to keep your notes for evidence).

Task 3

Produce a poster which **explains** the organisation and support required for **different types of meetings**. Your poster should include information on informal and formal meetings, internal and external meetings.

Task 4

You have been asked to provide all the required support for the meeting, including follow-up activities.

Your assessor will produce an observation statement to support your evidence.

Produce accurate and detailed post-meeting documentation, including minutes prepared from the notes you have taken during the meeting discussions. Please remember to include information on the monitoring of any actions identified during the meeting.

Your final tasks for this assignment are to produce a report which evaluates your own contribution to providing the support before, during and after the meeting, and to make suggestions on how to improve the tasks or activities that were weak.

Knowledge recap answers

Topic A.1

1. The administrator would need to know the location of the venue so they could book accommodation near the venue and find the most convenient way to travel there.
2. A set telephone procedure would ensure that all employees were using a consistent efficient response to all telephone calls.
3. The electronic diary can be shared by selected employees and this will make it easier to coordinate dates for meetings and visits. The diaries can be password protected and all entries can be backed up on a disk or a back-up file. The electronic diary can provide automatic alerts for forthcoming meetings or visits.

Topic A.2

1. A manager would rely on the business support process to organise and plan meetings, which would free them up to concentrate on more important issues. The business support team would be responsible for implementing processes which make the management process run more efficiently, such as easy access to filed documents; photocopying; producing clear and professional documents; and providing and relaying clear information for and from customers.
2. The business support process may be the first contact any potential or existing customer has with a business and it is important that customers are given a positive image of the business.

Topic B.1

1. The employees will gain a better understanding of all the features and functions for each piece of equipment and be able to use the equipment efficiently and safely.
2. Following the manufacturer's instructions will help to prevent the equipment being damaged and the cost of repair bills. Employees should be able to follow the instructions to help resolve minor problems. If the equipment is damaged the business may lose time waiting for parts or maintenance. Any incorrect use of the equipment could make any warranty worthless.
3. So that it is safe to use at all times; so that it can do the job it was purchased to do; so that it will last a long time and save money on repair bills

and replacement equipment; so that the manufacturer's warranty remains valid.

Topic B.2

1. The Health and Safety (Display Screen Equipment) Regulations 1992.
2. Using the correct techniques for lifting and moving heavy objects will help prevent injuries to the back, neck and shoulders.
3. A risk assessment is the identification of threats or risks to safety; to decide on the likelihood of threats/risks happening. The risk assessment will set a value of low to high on the likelihood of threats/risks happening and identify ways of reducing the likelihood of these happening. It will list the threats/risks in order of importance and decide which needs to be addressed first.

Topic C.1

1. The minutes of a meeting will not record any discussion or actions for items which are confidential.
2. The meeting will provide the opportunity for the employees to discuss the changes and the impact they will have on them. The meeting will provide the opportunity for the employees to highlight their concerns about the changes but will also help them feel more involved in the change process.

Topic C.2

1. The employee will be responsible for producing documents such as the agenda, minutes and attendance log. The employee will be responsible for arranging the venue, any equipment and refreshments. The employee will also be responsible for communicating information to all relevant staff and delegates.
2. The employee will need to know how much money is available for booking an external venue and for ordering resources and refreshments. The employee will need to ensure that any costs fall within the allocated budget.
3. The delegates will need to know the date and time of the meeting and the venue. The delegates will also need to know the agenda items so that they can prepare for the meeting. For an external meeting the delegates may need directions to the venue and information on transport and local accommodation.

Topic C.3

1. On the day of the meeting the employee will need a copy of the agenda, an attendance log sheet, spare copies of the minutes from the last meeting and any other materials which will be used during the meeting. The employee will also need a document on which to record notes for the minutes.

2. On the day of the meeting the person who organised the meeting would be responsible for:
   - arranging the room layout
   - checking that all the equipment is working
   - checking that the refreshments are available and when required serving the refreshments
   - welcoming delegates and issuing name badges
   - keeping an attendance log
   - making notes for the minutes.

3. The minutes are an accurate record of what was said and agreed without any bias or comment.

Topic C.4

1. The employee would be responsible for:
   - collecting in any documents which have been left by delegates or any spare copies
   - checking that the room is left clean and tidy
   - destroying any confidential documents
   - producing the minutes from the meeting.

2. The minutes should be an accurate record of the discussion and the agreed actions during the meeting. The chairperson should confirm that the minutes are an accurate record before they are distributed to the delegates.

3. The agreed actions should be monitored so that delegates can be provided with updates on progress made at the next meeting.

Picture credits

The authors and publishers would like to thank the following for the use of photographs in this volume:

Figure 1.1 © Sashkin – Fotolia; Figure 1.2 © Pakhnyushchyy – Fotolia; Figure 1.3 © Ingram Publishing Limited; Figure 1.4 © auremar – Fotolia; Figure 2.1 © Konstantin Shevtsov – Fotolia; Figure 2.2 © plus69free – Fotolia; Figure 2.3 © Dmitriy Melnikov – Fotolia; Figure 2.4 © stockimages – Fotolia; Figure 3.1 © chagin – Fotolia; Figure 3.2 © Sergey Nivens – Fotolia; Figure 3.3 © Robert Kneschke – Fotolia

Every effort has been made to trace and acknowledge ownership of copyright. The publishers will be glad to make suitable arrangements with any copyright holders whom it has not been possible to contact.